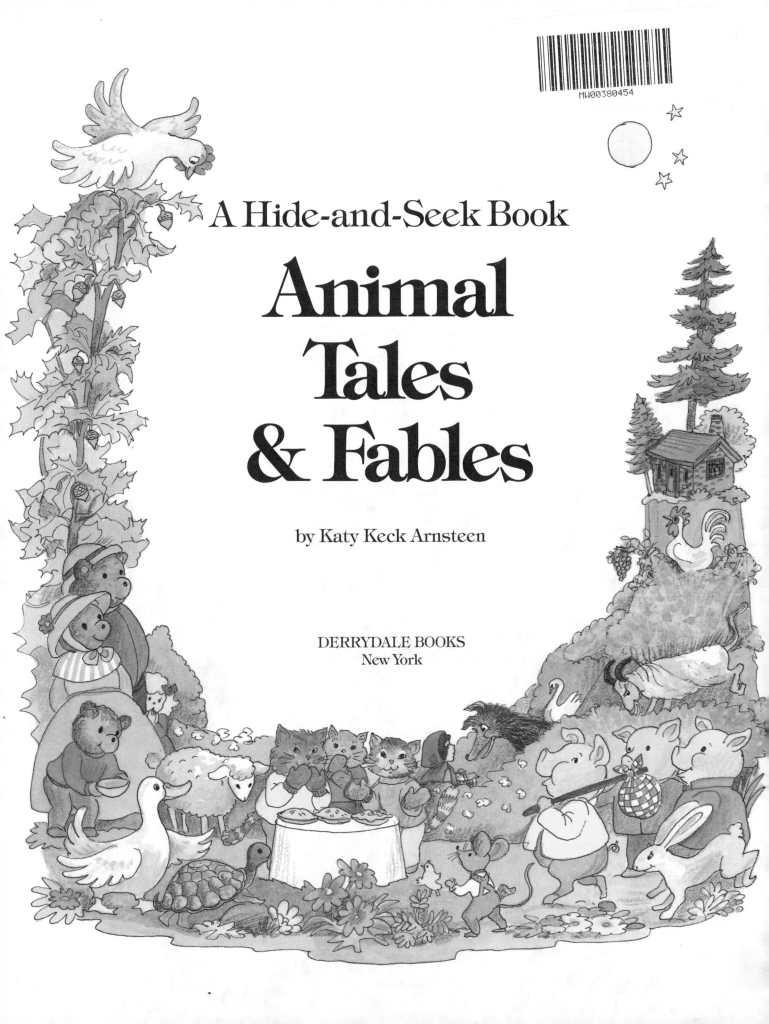

A Hide-and-Seek Book

Animal Tales & Fables

by Katy Keck Arnsteen

DERRYDALE BOOKS
New York

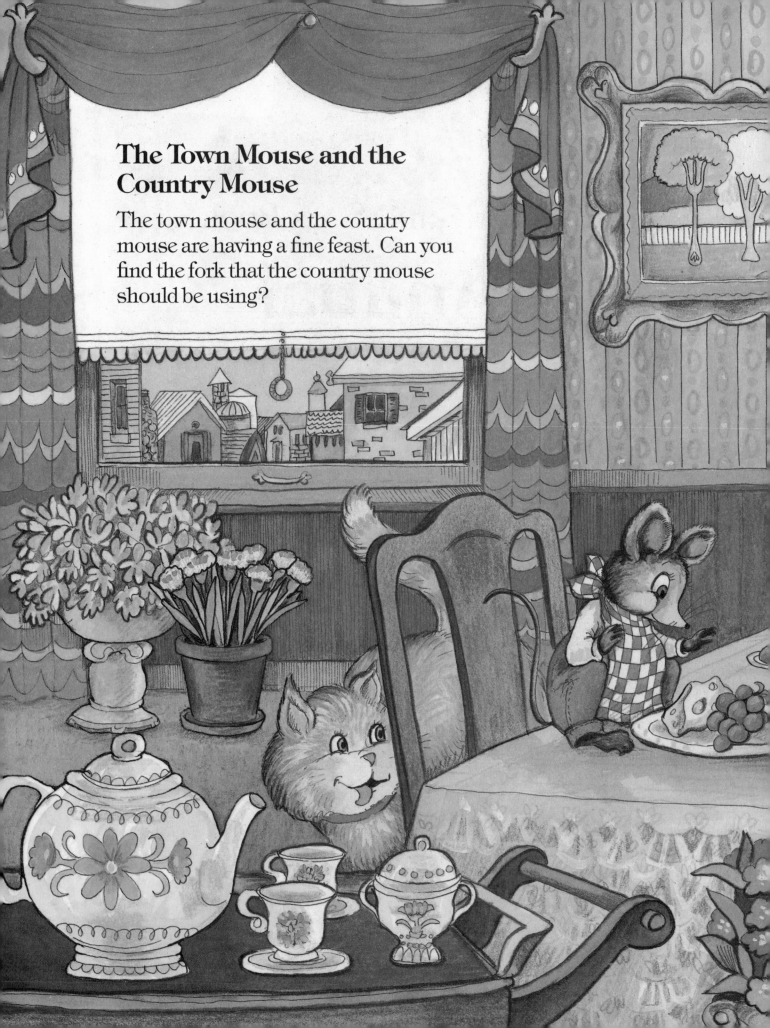

The Town Mouse and the Country Mouse

The town mouse and the country mouse are having a fine feast. Can you find the fork that the country mouse should be using?

The Tortoise and the Hare

The tortoise is going to pass the hare and win the race. Can you find the blue ribbon he will win?

Little Red Riding Hood

The wolf is pretending to be Red Riding Hood's grandmother, but he forgot one thing. Can you find the reading glasses that he should be wearing?

Chicken Little

An acorn has hit Chicken Little on the head,
and now she thinks the sky is falling! Can
you find the acorn?

The Little Boy
Who Cried "Wolf"

The little boy who shouted "wolf" lost his shepherd's staff. Can you find it?

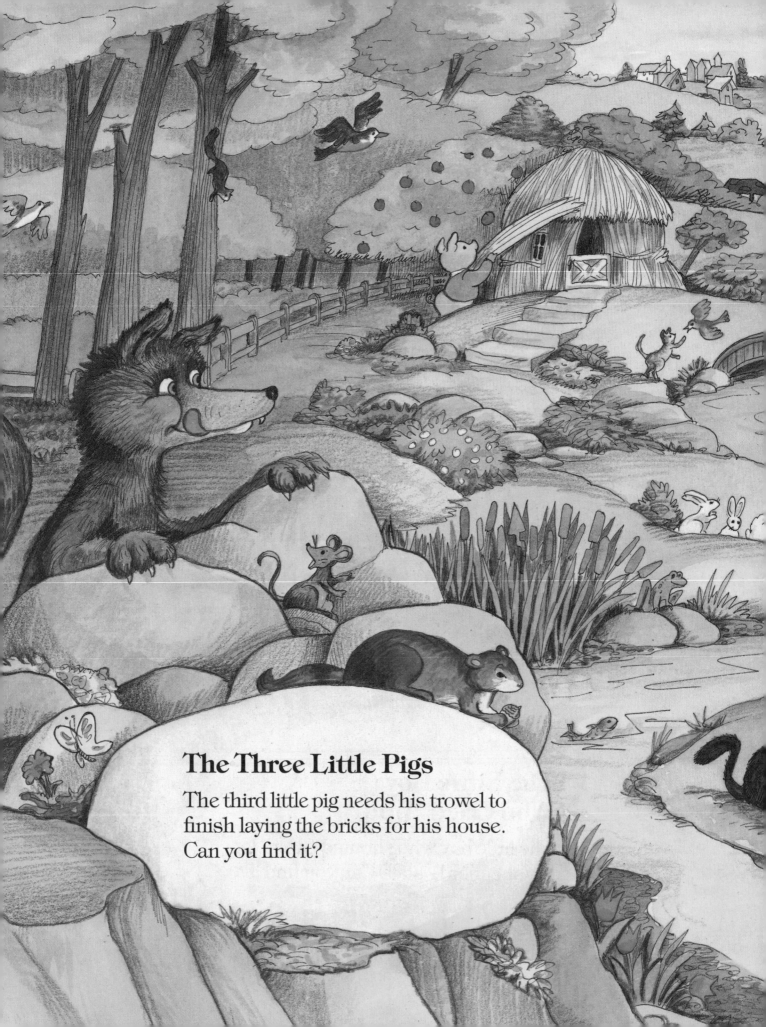

The Three Little Pigs

The third little pig needs his trowel to finish laying the bricks for his house. Can you find it?

The Ugly Duckling

The ugly duckling came from the same nest as the swans. Can you find the cracked egg it hatched from?

Goldilocks and the Three Bears

Goldilocks ate the porridge from baby bear's bowl. Can you find the empty bowl?

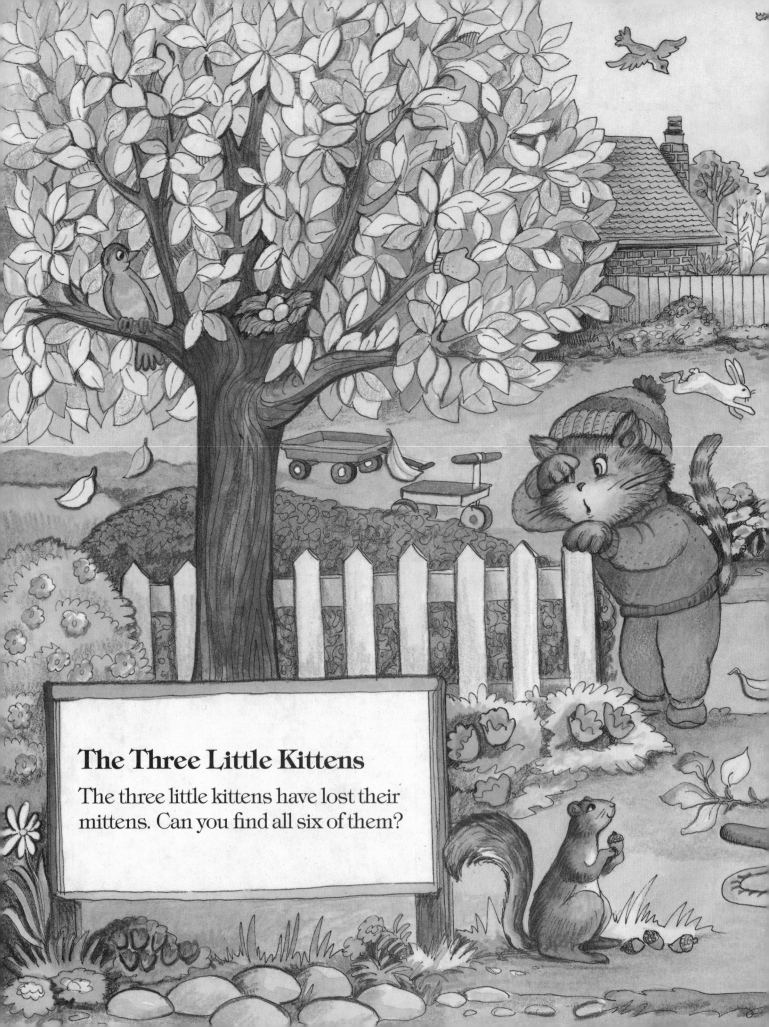

The Three Little Kittens

The three little kittens have lost their mittens. Can you find all six of them?

Three Billy Goats Gruff

When Big Billy Goat Gruff butted the troll off the bridge, the troll lost one of his boots. Can you find it?